CANADA COAST TO COAST

CANADA

PHOTOGRAPHY BY   *Paul von Baich   Wayne Barrett   Roméo Cormier*

Michael Drummond   Menno Fieguth   Owen Fitzgerald   Peter Fowler

Rudi Haas   Chic Harris   Anne MacKay   Michael Odesse   Hugo Redivo

Edith Robinson   Bill Simpkins   Robert R. Taylor   John de Visser

COAST TO COAST

INTRODUCTION BY *Roger Boulton*

TORONTO OXFORD UNIVERSITY PRESS 1982

CANADIAN CATALOGUING IN PUBLICATION DATA

Main entry under title:
Canada coast to coast

(Regional portraits of Canada)
ISBN 0-19-540388-6

1. Canada – Description and travel – 1950- -Views.*
I. Boulton, Roger, 1933-   II. Series.

FC59.C36   917.1′04646′0222   C82-094142-5
F1016.C36

Oxford University Press (Canadian Branch) 1982
ISBN 0-19-540388-6
1 2 3 4—5 4 3 2
Designed by Doug Frank
Printed in Hong Kong by
EVERBEST PRINTING COMPANY LIMITED

INTRODUCTION BY ROGER BOULTON

THIS BOOK grew out of several others—a whole series, in fact, about twenty books in all, each one an attempt to portray a particular place or region in Canada. They in turn derived from a personal experience. In 1965, being here on a year-long visit from Europe, I had the unusual opportunity, rarer then even than now, to travel by road across Canada, from coast to coast and back again. I travelled with my family, at leisure, with no deadlines to meet and no fixed route to follow. We took our time. We wandered off course for hundreds of miles here or there in any direction, staying in small roadside cottages or elaborate gothic hotels as occasion offered or as nightfall demanded after a long day's drive. When our journey ended three seasons had passed, and there were fifteen thousand miles more on our by-then beaten-up car. The night after our return my wife sat down to a dinner-party in Toronto and instinctively reached for the seat-belt on her chair.

The Trans-Canada Highway had been open for only three years. Few people had travelled its length. To most it was still a myth, romantic or daunting, depending on one's temperament. Quite a lot of consternation was expressed by friends in Toronto when we talked about our plans. We would need a second gas tank, they said, because gas stations were so few and far between. We would need a spare windshield because ours was bound to be shattered by stones flying up from the prairie roads.

We would be snow-bound in the mountains, and had better take supplies of dried food, and of course a set of chains. I began to think of the time long before when I left England for India and asked my old headmaster, 'Do you think, sir, I should take a revolver?' He looked at me blandly and said, 'If I were you, Boulton, I should take a coffin.'

Nobody seemed to think a trip across Canada to be a very practical idea, but that wasn't surprising. I had already found in the first few weeks we spent in Toronto that the city people knew little of the country around them, apart from places like Muskoka where they holidayed in the summer. Toronto in those days was nothing like the size it is now, just a large pleasant town with a very domestic character. We were able to rent a furnished house in Rosedale for very little money. The old St Lawrence Market buildings housed a bustling crowd of farmers as yet undiscovered by fashion. At Don Mills the open fields began. The Beaver Valley was largely unknown. Up there wandering cows looked out at us from the windows of tumbling farmhouses. The Caledon Hills were still so rural that you might sit and picnic on a rock and only realize when you came to clear away the crumbs that you'd been sharing sun and shade with a family of snakes. There were no ski-lifts yet at Hockley. The untouched shore of Cape Croker was like the abandoned garden of a giant. The road system then was nothing like it is today.

There is a story that when the Bruce Trail was being mapped out in Ontario, a couple of hikers, prospecting it, came to the edge of an impassable ravine. Deep in the fields at its base a man was tending his cabbages. They hollered down, 'Can you tell us how to get to the other side?' He hollered back, 'No, I was born down here.' An apocryphal story no doubt, but certainly distance as much as language or cultural heritage has, I believe, always formed the greatest gulf between Canadians. Even if they remotely share a common ancestry, how can a man whose family have farmed for generations the temperate fields along Lake Ontario understand a New-foundlander whose parents and great-grandparents fought the Labrador Current from tiny villages perched on cliffs where it might seem that only seabirds could survive? How can either of them know the feelings of those who grew up in the boundless steppes of the central prairies where only the cloud formations mediate between man and infinity? These different Canadians can truly understand each other only, one would suppose, if they can travel and meet, and each see how the other lives.

We at least were blessed with total ignorance. We knew absolutely nothing about Canada, except what little could be read from the map. We would go west to the Pacific, travel back east to the Atlantic, and then return to Toronto. To us as Europeans, the distances seemed immense. Two hundred miles was a lot. Four thousand was so much as not to bother us any the more. The first day out from Toronto we aimed to go only as far as Gravenhurst. I still remember stepping out onto the verandah of our little motel at Gull Lake on that first evening, between tall scented pines, and looking at the shimmer of the water. A few little golden windows winked across from the farther shore. This must be what they meant in Toronto by 'Cottage Country'.

It was at Sudbury or North Bay that I first began to get some idea of what North American paintings were all about. Until then their colours had always seemed harsh, crude, crazy almost, as though the painters didn't know what they were doing. I had been raised on misty landscapes inspired by the ceaseless shifting weathers of England and the Ile de France. Now for the first time I saw the blue of an empty North American sky and its brilliant sun on red brick houses, in the still moment of an early Sunday morning. The painters were right. Their light was true.

We pushed on, through Blind River, past the first big waterfalls and the first edge of forest, to Sault Ste Marie, fascinated by the architecture, which seemed to us so strange, so lively, so informal. We rounded a bend in the road, cut through massive cliffs of pre-Cambrian granite, and came suddenly upon the glory of Lake Superior. Perhaps it was an echo of the Greek name Thessalon lingering in my mind, but ever afterwards I always thought of that coastline as being classical, Homeric in its grandeur.

Seagulls in the morning fog at Batchawana Bay, interested in the fish that we were cooking for breakfast on the pebble shore; great islands, so many of them and nameless to us, out in the glittering midday vastness of the lake. At White River it was cold at night, as the locals proudly proclaimed it would be. Our motel had a heated indoor pool surrounded by Hawaian greenery, but outside in the frigid air I sat for hours on the roadside watching the transcontinental truck lights grow from the far western distance to shudder roaring past me, leaving the northern silence to settle again.

We travelled slowly, with many side trips, to places like Helen Lake and Beardmore, or into the forests to look at amethyst deposits, or out to a ghost town left by silver miners, so that when we reached Port Arthur and Fort William we had been on the road for nearly a week. Already we had begun to know the few others like us who were travelling the highway. We would meet at a look-out point, chat, and then come across each other again a day or two later. Some of these people we kept meeting off and on like that for thousands of miles, into the Rockies and even beyond. A comradeship developed befitting fellow passengers on a long voyage.

Across the waters of Thunder Bay we sensed what yet lay before us, foretold in the magnificence of a sunset seen from Sibley Point. No other ever outshone its blaze and splendour. We stood amazed on the high cliffs, while flocks of gulls flew far below along the shoreline, and moose fed at the edge of a pond in the wood at our back. This sunset was our first promise of the West. To reach it we had to travel another day, leaving Kakabeka Falls, the 'Niagara of the North', and plunging into what seemed an endless tunnel of forest. We drove through Keewatin and Kenora and Lake of the Woods until at last the trees became smaller and sparser, and the forests opened out to reveal the prairie and the sky. Not just a flat, straight road, telegraph poles ranking down in mathematical order, but a pure space that made us look up and around us as never before, and a clarity that defined every golden stalk of grain to the farthest limit of vision. Fragments of the human past were intimate and close. An old car outside a worn white frame house stood as though preserved by the prairie light for generations.

We learned the harshness of the prairie climate. In the tiny block-built hospital at Beauséjour we left part of our selves in exchange for the care that saved our three-year-old son from dying of dehydration. We rested at Dauphin, a little Ukrainian town with backyards full of sunflowers grown by the farmers who worked the great black fields around. Then through the Battlefords, by the wandering magnificence of the South Saskatchewan

River, through Yorkton, Saskatoon, and Lethbridge. By the time we crossed into Alberta we had come to love the northern prairie towns, so kind, so varied, gathering into them the listening vastness of the land.

Our first sight of Edmonton was appropriately the glitter of oil towers glimpsed through a thick mass of corn ripe for harvest. Even we could sense the power and wealth of this city of flaring refineries and grandiose government buildings, a city poised at the crossroads of great national routeways high on the cliffs above a splendid river. Already impatient for the mountains, we hurried on. From Edmonton to Jasper is a long way, and the approach to the Rockies at this point is slow and undramatic. They do not surge up from the plains as they do outside Calgary, like symphonic thunder. They emerged tentatively as individual blue peaks seen down firelanes cut through the forests, until suddenly we were among them, driving along the foot of the Palisades, across the stony shallows of the Athabasca River.

The glaciers have receded a lot in recent years. There are walkways now, with guardrails, signposts, tearooms, and less of the sense of a new Himalaya, or as Ruskin described his first sight of the Alps, 'the seen walls of lost Eden.' The campgrounds are packed in summer; bears and deer are less likely to come up to your cabin windows; but the lakes will always be that startling, unbelievable turquoise blue. In Banff we came across our first red-coated Mountie, wearing his Baden-Powell hat and his breeches and boots. He wasn't engaged in any musical ride, wasn't playing a bit-part to some politician's self-importance. He was just quietly walking his beat outside one of the many small churches that graced this little hill-town, which seemed to me for all the world like another Darjeeling.

After the build-up we had been given in Toronto, the Rogers Pass, like Hell's Gate on the Fraser Canyon later, was very much an anti-climax. The road across the Rockies at this point had been so superbly engineered that we did not even know we were over until we stopped and looked back in awe at the white ranges behind us. We gazed in wonder over the Selkirks, then wound down the Fraser and the Thompson, passing small tumbled wooden corrals and tiny pioneer churches abandoned beneath towering cliffs. Somewhere on the Thompson a cowboy rode by, dusty, slung with ammunition belt, saddle holster, rifle and all. I was so startled that I nearly drove off the road. Was he real or just a figment of my tired imagination? Everywhere we sensed the past, a wholly western past, with a certain sadness epitomized by the broken fragments of wooden irrigation pipes on the dry sage slopes at Walhachin. Here peaches had flourished and a settlement had grown until the First World War, when all the men went to Flanders, and by the time any survivors returned it was too late. Few people realize that

Canada includes a true patch of wild western desert. The Okanagan, part of the great Central Basin that runs south to Colorado, was once a true desert of rattlesnakes and sage brush and now is rich with blossoms, fruit, and vines. We came over the last range and down to Hope, well named, peaceful between great avenues of misty firs, a place to rest before the final stretch to the sea.

Vancouver is now one of the most visited spots in Canada. Then it was still remote, and the Island, outside Victoria, even more so. Vancouver had little cosmopolitanism as yet, other than the mix of languages and faces that you find in any seaport. No chic, no highrise, no urban renewal—just a friendly place of docks and lumber, beautifully surrounded by the mountains and the sea. We walked among the sodden autumn leaves of Stanley Park and watched the freighters waiting out at sea over the weekend. A Russian vessel came in from Vladivostok. We had reached the Pacific.

Over on Vancouver Island we met a retired stockbroker from Montreal who sat on the floor of his fishing cabin drunkenly repeating half the night, 'This is Camelot, this is Camelot.' Certainly the view from his cabin across the Strait of Georgia was the landscape of a legend, with the mainland mountains rising above the islands of Lasceti and Texada.

Victoria was a town of whimsy, an odd blend of slightly absurd anglo-Indian raj mixed with the endearing casualness common to sea people and westerners alike. In Oak Bay we rented a cottage by a duck-pond with a lawn stretching to the shore. When I knocked down the end wall of the little garage with my big station-wagon, the landlord wasn't at all dismayed. It had happened before, he said, and there was plenty of driftwood on the beach—so all it cost me was a day's work with planks pulled back from the sand. It did cut down our sightseeing time, though. We never got across to the limitless rollers of Long Beach, later to become Pacific Rim National Park.

It was hard to turn around and start back east again. Calgary seemed to pass us by. We were exhausted and distracted, after a terrifying struggle with a blizzard high in the passes of the Kootenays. By the time we got down, our car was covered with a thick blanket of frozen mud that took days to thaw out and we felt as miserable as the cattle wintering in the relentless snow. It wasn't till several years afterwards that I came to enjoy Calgary, which by then had spread out, brawny and glittering at night as far as the eye could see.

Back again in central Canada, we found that after the West all our perceptions had changed. What before had been so strange to us as Europeans now seemed familiar. Countryside that only three months earlier had seemed empty now felt crowded. Ontario appeared to be as thickly woven with small historic towns and villages as southern England or Holland or Northern France. It had taken the western experience to make us appreciate the history of the east. Only by knowing the wilderness, even for such a little while, could one guess at the courage of those who had first left the relative securities of New France or the Canadas to make their way along the river routes, or by railroad, through the forests to the West.

In Ottawa we found that the fantasy of Westminster Palace and the Albert Memorial had evidently floated around the world a century before, giving rise in Bombay to what we used to call PWD (Public Works Department) Gothic, and in a tiny sawmill town on the border of French and English Canada to that most romantic achievement, the complex of Parliament Hill. We enjoyed the Edwardian luxury of a great railway hotel, the Château Laurier, and in complete contrast the village simplicity of the Byward street market one block away. We had our first glimpses of Eskimo art, a new excitement for us.

Before we had left Toronto, I naively asked somebody, 'What kind of cigarettes do they smoke in Quebec?', and sure enough the answer had been, 'The same as we do of course—Canadian, eh?' It struck me as strange to assume that the French would not have their own brands, but they didn't, and crossing into Quebec one was conscious of little change at first—the towns somewhat poorer, perhaps depressed. The great regeneration of

Quebec was yet to come. In the years since then we have talked a lot in the rest of Canada about 'identity', but the Québécois have acted to claim it and define it for themselves.

Inevitably growth and change have had their losses as well as their gains. Montreal is a great city that in physical terms seems almost wilfully to have destroyed itself. Alone of the big towns of North America, Montreal had maintained into this century a splendid tradition of architecture in the local stone, the great seminaries, the hundreds of churches, the squares, terraces, and mansions of a bourgeoisie as wealthy as any. All periods and styles existed together, from seventeenth-century French to nineteenth-century baroque. Now most of them are gone. Belatedly Montreal has turned to restoring and preserving its past; but so little remains that, although I have come to love the city and often stay there, I cannot visit it without thinking of what has been lost.

Further down the St Lawrence time lost is time regained. Old Quebec itself may be the most perfect French city of the period left in any place, including France herself, and the French spoken there is still the clear, pure language of Racine. Like all European cities of old, and unlike almost any other in North America, Quebec is a place to walk and simply enjoy the beauty of the streets. Seen across the green lawns of the Citadel ramparts, the white house-fronts of the Rue Saint-Denis shone like jewels. Winding down into the Lower Town, I could almost think myself in the Latin Quarter of Paris thirty years back, before the cars took over. From the Citadel the sweep of the St Lawrence past Lévis presented a panorama hardly changed at all since Morrice painted it at the turn of the century. The St Lawrence below Quebec has a grandeur with which few rivers in the world compare.

Going on down the river below Montmorency Falls and through the exquisite rural charm of the Ile d'Orleans, we made the great roller-coaster ride, plunging and rising with the hills of the North Shore through tiny spired villages, their saints' names richly eloquent. We ferried across the river and drove south into the Maritimes, where autumn was giving way to winter as the cathedral of Fredericton rose through the mist. Massive breakers pounded the red stone cliffs of Prince Edward Island. At evening the farmhouse windows flashed back a golden sunlight over miles of scarlet furrows under purple wind-swept skies. The hillsides of Nova Scotia were scarlet also, with the dying leaves of wild berries, and in the fishing villages of the south shore the boats and lobster traps and wooden buoys had all been pulled up out of reach of the coming storms. On the Cabot Trail we were caught in dense fog and it was thankfully that we rounded the Cape Breton Highlands and came south again to Louisbourg, where the first snows of

winter were drifting in from the North Atlantic across the ruins of what once had been the mightiest fortress on the continent.

We arrived in St John's, at the easternmost point of the Americas, nearer once more to Europe than to the West that we had left so far behind. The wind was fierce. The snow blew straight in flat lines across our windows up on Signal Hill all night long. In the morning the sun shone but the city was snow-bound. Nothing could move except on foot. The streets were deep in snow, the cars covered in drifts. The red, yellow, blue, black, lime-green fronts of the clapboard houses glowed brilliantly against the white. There was no noise, no sound at all but the laughter of children playing snowball. Stepping down into Water Street, I felt myself taken back to the Christmas morning of a Dickens' novel. By midday it was all over. The snowplows had done their work. The cars and buses were rumbling around again. I was back in my own time, but for a moment I had been allowed to glimpse the town as it must have been on any winter's day a hundred years before.

Newfoundland is endlessly rich in language, legends, stories of heroism, extraordinary conjunctions of culture—one of the greatest folk heritages left in North America. But now the oil has been found, the outports are being closed, the 'white fleet' has gone, and all is changing fast. On that first morning in St John's, as the snow was cleared away, with it went the illusion of escape to a past that was simpler and gentler than the present.

Looking back afterwards, that snowy morning in St John's seemed symbolic. I have sometimes wondered since if a large part of our impressions all along had been illusions. After the wars and discontents of Europe, it seemed for much of the journey that we had discovered a country so blessed by nature and history that its people had no other problems than to live out satisfying, straightforward lives. There was stability and, so it seemed, contentment—no Berlin wall, but rather an open road across a continent; no secret armies, but rather an innocence of politics; no hunger, but rather a wealth of produce in every market; no slums, but towns of tree-lined streets; no refugees sleeping in desperation on railway platforms, but family picnics that brought together scores of relatives and several generations every year.

Were we merely foreigners projecting our own longings onto a country that we hardly knew at all and still less understood? Not entirely so. In truth Canada then was home to immense and justifiable hopes. The highway that Canadians had built from coast to coast offered a promise of freedom and of understanding between the many peoples of this diverse land. Much has changed since, with many disappointments and divisions among us, but the possibilities remain. The highway is still there waiting for us, just outside the door.

Toronto 1982

1 Hampton, Prince Edward Island

2   Gathering Irish moss in the National Park, Prince Edward Island
3   Cavendish, Prince Edward Island

4 Cabot Park, Malpeque, Prince Edward Island

5   Emyvale, Prince Edward Island

6   Victoria, Prince Edward Island

7 Kings Landing Historical Settlement,
Kings Landing, New Brunswick

8   Christ Church Cathedral (1845-53), Fredericton, New Brunswick

9   Officers' quarters, Military Compound (1839-69), Fredericton, New Brunswick

10 Saint-Joseph-de-Madawaska,
New Brunswick

11   St John River near Sheffield, New Brunswick

12   Estuary of St John River from the Martello Tower, Saint John, New Brunswick

13   Cabot Trail winding around Cap Rouge, Cape Breton, Nova Scotia

14 Lunenburg, Nova Scotia

15   Peggy's Cove, Nova Scotia

16   L'Habitation, reconstructed as in the early 1600s, Port Royal, Nova Scotia

17   Chapel of Our Lady of Sorrows, 'the Chapel built in a day' (1843), Halifax, Nova Scotia

18   St John's Church (1754),
      Lunenburg, Nova Scotia

19   Fortress of Louisbourg, reconstructed as in the early 1740s, Cape Breton, Nova Scotia

20   Historic Properties, Halifax, Nova Scotia

21   Halifax Harbour, looking towards Dartmouth, Nova Scotia

22 Oil-rig under construction, Halifax, Nova Scotia
23 Old Town Clock (1803), Halifax, Nova Scotia

24   Dawn over Signal Hill and the Narrows, St John's, Newfoundland
25   Gower Street, St John's, Newfoundland

26   Bonne Bay, Newfoundland

27   Burin, Newfoundland

28 Harbour le Cou, Newfoundland

29 Trout River, Newfoundland

30 Dog-sled near Nain, Labrador

31   Iles-de-la-Madeleine, Quebec

32   Calving iceberg in the Labrador Current

33 Percé Rock, Quebec

34 La Malbaie, Quebec
35 Snow-geese migration at Cap-Tourmente, Quebec

36   Low tide at Bic, Quebec
37   Sainte-Anne-de-Beaupré
      from the Ile d'Orléans, Quebec

38   Quebec City seen from the
St Lawrence River, Quebec
39   Montmorency Falls, Quebec

40   Rue Saint-Denis from the Citadel, Quebec City, Quebec

41   Dufferin Terrace and the Citadel, Quebec City, Quebec

42 Notre-Dame-des-Victoires
(1688), Place Royale,
Quebec City, Quebec

43 Rue de la Montagne from
Montmorency Park,
Quebec City, Quebec

44 Wolfe-Montcalm Monument,
Governor's Garden,
Quebec City, Quebec

45 Montreal, Quebec,
from Mont Royal,
with Mont Saint-Bruno
and Mont Saint-Hilaire
in the background

46 Tower of the Sailor's Chapel,
Notre-Dame-de-Bonsecours
(1773; remodelled 1886-92),
Montreal, Quebec
47 Main altar, Notre-Dame-de-
Montréal (1824-8),
Montreal, Quebec

48   Wedding, Mary Queen of the World Basilica, Montreal, Quebec

49 Bonsecours Market (begun 1844), Montreal, Quebec

50   Saint-Antoine-sur-Richelieu, Quebec

51   Saint-François-d'Assise-de-Beauce Church, Beauceville, Quebec

52   Mount Orford, Eastern Townships, Quebec

53　Abbey of Saint-Benoit-du-Lac, overlooking
Lake Memphremagog, Quebec

54   Near Boucherville, Quebec
55   Gathering maple syrup, Saint-Janvier, Quebec

58   The Rideau Canal, Ottawa
59   The Rideau Canal at night, with silhouettes of the National Arts
      Centre, the Parliament Buildings and the Conference Centre, Ottawa

60 Sculpture at the base of the
Samuel de Champlain
monument, Nepean Point,
Ottawa

61   Manotick, Ontario

62   The Parliament Buildings from Nepean Point, Ottawa
63   St Lawrence Islands, near Ivylea, Ontario

64   Dining room, Cook's Tavern, Upper Canada Village,
       Morrisburg, Ontario
65   Outside Cook's Tavern, Upper Canada Village, Morrisburg, Ontario

66 Gananoque, Ontario
67 The Brimley House,
   Grafton, Ontario

68 Royal Military College
   (1876), Kingston, Ontario
69 Kingston, Ontario

70   Port Hope, Ontario

71   The Marie Dressler House (restored to c. 1830), Cobourg, Ontario

72 Near Warkworth, Ontario
73 Toronto, Ontario, the
 harbour seen from the
 Eastern Gap

74 Nathan Phillips Square with the Old City Hall (1891-9), Toronto, Ontario

75   Union Station, Toronto, Ontario

76   The Royal York Hotel, Toronto, Ontario

77 Eaton Centre, Toronto, Ontario

78 Ontario Hydro Building,
Toronto, Ontario
79 Centre Island, Toronto, Ontario

80   St Lawrence Market, Toronto, Ontario

81   Caribana Festival, Toronto, Ontario

82　Knox College (1915), University of Toronto, Toronto, Ontario

83 Drawing room,
Dundurn Castle (1832-4),
Hamilton, Ontario

84 House of William Lyon Mackenzie (1795-1861), Queenston, Ontario, where he founded *The Colonial Advocate* in 1824

85 Prince of Wales Hotel, Niagara-on-the-Lake, Ontario

86   Skylon Tower and Horseshoe Falls,
Niagara, Ontario

87   Welland Canal, Ontario

88 Dawn, south of London, Ontario

89   Town Hall (1851-2),
       Woodstock, Ontario

90   St Andrew's United Church, London, Ontario

91   Near Wingham, Ontario

92 Elora, Ontario
93 Elgin County, Ontario

94   Mennonites on their way to church, Waterloo County, Ontario

95   Kincardine, Ontario

96 Festival Theatre, Stratford, Ontario
97 Point Pelee, Ontario, southernmost tip of
    the Canadian mainland

98 Trilliums, Balls Falls
Conservation Area, Ontario,
99 Little Hawk Lake, Ontario

100 Sainte-Marie among the Hurons, a reconstruction of the Jesuit
     mission (1639-49) that was the first inland European settlement
     in North America, near Midland, Ontario

101 Summer home at Roches
Point on Lake Simcoe, Ontario

102　Burleigh Falls, Kawartha Lakes, Ontario

103　Dawn, Algonquin Park, Ontario

104   Trans-Canada Highway, north of Sault Ste Marie, Ontario
105   Near Heyden, Ontario

106   Lake Nipissing, Ontario

107   Sudbury, Ontario

109   Near Terrace Bay, Ontario

110   Mission Bay, Helen Lake, Ontario
111   Old Woman Bay, Lake Superior, Ontario

112   Spring stubble fires, near Clandeboye, Manitoba

113   Whitemouth, Manitoba

114   Portage and Main, Winnipeg, Manitoba

115   Grave of Louis Riel (1844-85), with St Boniface Cathedral (1908),
       Winnipeg, Manitoba

116 Great gray owl, Spruce Siding, Manitoba
117 Moose, Eastern Manitoba

118 Ukrainian dancers, Dauphin, Manitoba
119 Wood Mountain, Saskatchewan

120 Confluence of the North Saskatchewan and Battle Rivers, near
the Battlefords, Saskatchewan

121 Harvesting along the North Saskatchewan River, near Baljennie, Saskatchewan

122 Legislative Building (1908-12), Regina, Saskatchewan
123 RCMP Musical Ride, Saskatoon, Saskatchewan

124 Saskatoon, with the South Saskatchewan River, Saskatchewan

125   North Saskatchewan River near Paynton, Saskatchewan

126   Weyburn and the Souris River, Saskatchewan

127 Father Albert Lacombe's Chapel (1861), St Albert, Alberta

128   Edmonton, Alberta

129   Yellowhead Highway, near Jasper, Alberta

130 Athabasca River, at Jasper, Alberta
131 Edmonton, Alberta, with the Muttart Conservatory

132   Mt Robson, near Tête-Jaune Cache, British Columbia
133   Guest Ranch at Mt Robson, British Columbia

134 Cascade area,
    Southern Alberta
135 Angel Glacier,
    Mt Edith Cavell, Alberta

136   Bow Glacier, Alberta
137   The Needles,
        above Lake Louise, Alberta

138   Banff Avenue, Banff, Alberta
139   Banff Springs Hotel, Banff, Alberta

140   Macleod Trail, Calgary, Alberta

141   Downtown Calgary, Alberta

142 Chuckwagon race, Calgary
Exhibition and Stampede,
Calgary, Alberta

143 Round-up, Lone Star Ranch
Jumping Pound, Alberta

144 Coalhurst, Alberta
145 Rosebud, Alberta

146 Prince of Wales Hotel,
Waterton, Alberta
147 Saint Patrick's Roman
Catholic Church, Medicine
Hat, Alberta

148 Medicine Man, Indian Days,
    near Stand-Off, Alberta
149 Dinosaur Provincial Park,
    Brooks, Alberta

150   Sternwheeler *S.S. Moyie*, Kaslo, British Columbia

151 Skaha Lake in the Okanagan Valley, British Columbia

152   Helmcken Falls, Wells Gray Provincial Park, British Columbia

153 'Ksan Indian Village, near Hazelton, British Columbia

154   Yellowhead Route near Terrace, British Columbia
155   Looking west from Haines Road, km 80, British Columbia

156   Hudson Bay coast, Churchill, Manitoba

157   Polar Bear, Churchill, Manitoba

158　Aurora Borealis, Yukon

159   Faber Lake, Northwest Territories

160   Ogilvie Mountains, Yukon

161 Kluane National Park, Yukon

Pangnirtung, Northwest Territories

163   Chilkoot Pass, British Columbia

164 *Inukshuks,* Pelly Bay, Northwest Territories
165 Inuit woman cleaning arctic char with an *ulu,* Northwest Territories.

168   Tatshenshini River, Yukon
169   Fraser River near Yale,
      British Columbia

170   Vancouver, British Columbia, from Queen Elizabeth Park

171   North Vancouver with the North Shore Mountains, British Columbia

172   Vancouver, British Columbia, from Stanley Park
173   Burrard Street, Vancouver, British Columbia

174   Annual Sandcastle Competition, White Rock, British Columbia

175 Stanley Park, Vancouver, British Columbia

176   Deep Cove, Indian Arm, British Columbia

177   False Creek, Vancouver, British Columbia

178   Cathedral Grove, Macmillan Provincial Park, Port Alberni, British Columbia

179 Active Pass with Mayne Island, from Galiano, British Columbia

180 British Columbia Parliament
     Buildings (1898), Victoria,
     British Columbia
181 The Empress Hotel (1905),
     Victoria, British Columbia

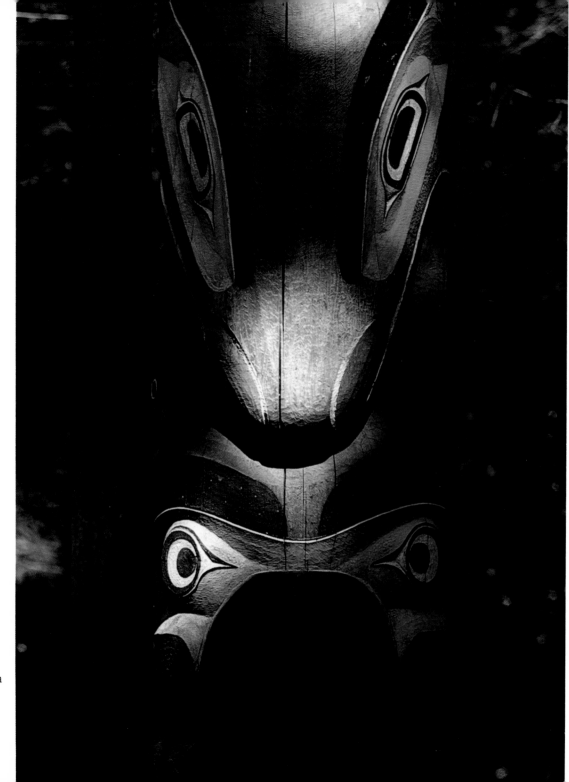

184   Lion's Gate Bridge, Vancouver, British Columbia

185 Sunset over the Coastal Mountains near Vancouver, British Columbia

186　Comber's Beach, Pacific Rim
National Park,
British Columbia

ACKNOWLEDGEMENTS

The Publishers wish to thank the photographers for their permission to use the images published in this book. The plate numbers of their contributions are listed below.

PAUL VON BAICH 38, 41, 44, 46, 49, 63, 66-72, 104-111, 150, 155, 158-161, 163, 168, 169, 181-183 WAYNE BARRETT 1, 3-9, 15, 20, 22-23 ROMÉO CORMIER 10 MICHAEL DRUMMOND 45, 50, 54, 55 MENNO FIEGUTH 119-126, 170-180, 184-186 OWEN FITZGERALD 13, 19 PETER FOWLER 84-87, 98, 99, 101 RUDI HAAS 56-62 CHIC HARRIS 14, 16-18 ANNE MACKAY 11, 12 MICHAEL ODESSE 100 HUGO REDIVO 151 EDITH ROBINSON 2 BILL SIMPKINS 129, 131, 133, 134, 136-149 ROBERT R. TAYLOR 112-118, 156, 157 JOHN DE VISSER 21, 24-37, 39, 40, 42, 43, 47, 48, 51-53, 64, 65, 73-83, 88-97, 102, 103, 127, 128, 130, 132, 135, 152-154, 162, 164-167